Junio Road Riaer

Second Edition

Written by Leila Kirk
Illustrated by Maggie Raynor

The Pony Club
Stoneleigh Park
Kenilworth
Warwickshire
CV8 2RW

Website: www.pcuk.org

First published in the UK in 2001
Revised edition 2005
Second revised edition 2009
Reprinted with revised cover 2010

British Library Cataloguing-in-Publication Data
A catalogue record for this book
is available from the British Library

ISBN 978-0-9561071-0-1

Edited and produced by Barbara Cooper
Designed and typeset by Hugh Johnson
Printed in Great Britain by Halstan & Co.

Trade distribution by Kenilworth Press
An imprint of Quiller Publishing Ltd
Wykey House, Wykey, Shrewsbury, SY4 1JA
Tel: 01939 261616 Fax: 01939 261606
E-mail: info@quillerbooks.com
Website: www.kenilworthpress.co.uk

Contents

Be Seen to Be Safe

Be safe before you set off by preparing and checking your pony and tack carefully.

Is your pony happy? Check that he is sound and well. Make sure that his shoes are not loose.

Do you think that you might fall off? There are three important things you can do to prevent this.

● Help your pony to behave. Always talk to him in a calm way, especially when you are in traffic or near something scary.

● If he does not always stop when you ask him to, have a few lessons before riding out. *The Highway Code* says that before you take your horse or pony onto the road you should be able to control it.

● If your pony is not used to roads, ride out with a friend who has a calm horse. Or tell your mother that cycling with you will do her legs the world of good!! Make sure that she also wears her high visibility clothing.

Make sure that your tack is safe.

When you clean your tack, check for big cracks **(1)** and loose stitches **(2)**, especially stirrup leathers and reins. If some items are too damaged to be mended, new ones will be necessary.

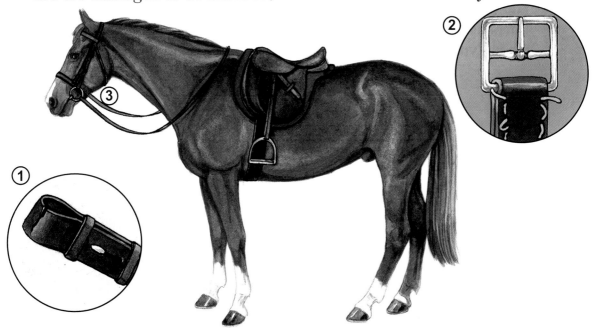

Make sure that your tack is fastened correctly.
Remember to fasten the throat lash **(3)**. Don't leave it dangling - which is what can happen when the reins have been twisted through it and then taken out.

Check the girth **(4)** before you mount, when you have mounted, and before you leave the yard. Ponies are really good at keeping their tummies puffed out for ages!

Dress to be safe

All riding hats (**1**) must comply with current regulations and must be labelled with a quality symbol such as the BSI Kite Mark. If you are under fourteen years old, by law your hat must be fastened with a three-pointed harness (straps that form a triangle over your ears.) Check your hat regularly for any wear and tear.

If your pony snatches at his bit - to go faster, to eat grass or to simply mess about - you will find it necessary to wear gloves (**2**). As well as preventing the reins from hurting your fingers, they also provide extra grip. Light-coloured gloves show up well when you are giving signals. Many young people make the mistake of riding in footwear without heels, such as trainers. This is dangerous, as your feet can slip through the stirrups and get stuck (**3**). If your pony shies, rears or slips, and you are thrown, your feet will need to come out of the stirrups immediately.

Wear jodhpur or riding boots, or lace-up shoes with proper heels (**4**).

Be noticeable before you set out. Make sure that you and your pony can be seen.

A rider in a dark coat on a bay pony can be difficult to see, even on a sunny day. Wear clothes that show up: e.g. fluorescent jackets and reflective bands. Fluorescent clothing is a bright greeny yellow, which shows up well in daylight.

Reflective bands are also useful on dull and rainy days, as they show up when car headlights shine on them.

This drawing shows all the different types of reflective clothing that can be worn by you and your pony.

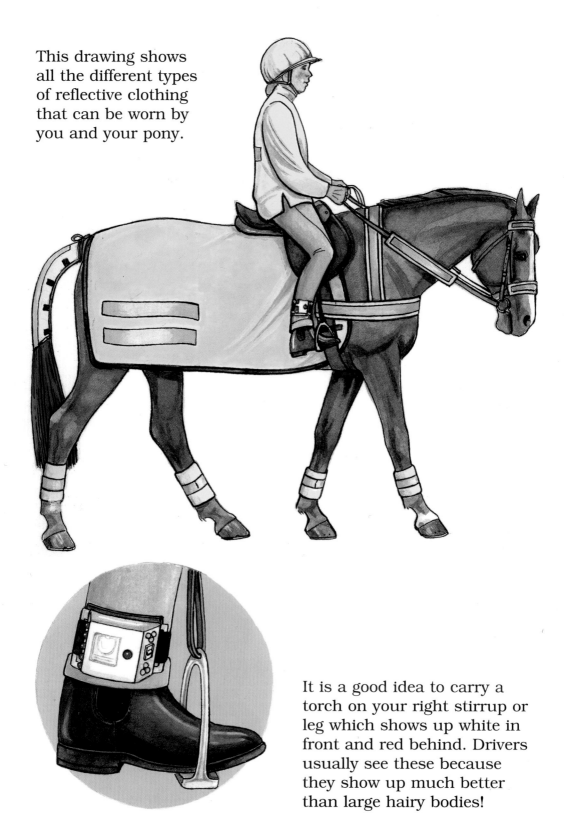

It is a good idea to carry a torch on your right stirrup or leg which shows up white in front and red behind. Drivers usually see these because they show up much better than large hairy bodies!

Even when you are only leading your pony you should still wear bright clothes. In fading light you should carry either a torch or a twinkling red light (as used by cyclists) on your right arm - which is the arm nearest to the middle of the road.

On dull and rainy days it is more difficult for car drivers to see you, so you must be sure to wear the correct clothes. Remember also that when it is wet the roads are slippery for your pony and for the cars as they try to slow down for you.

Know before you go: plan your ride.

There are two good reasons for planning where to go before you set off. They are:

1. To let other people in the yard or at home know where you are and when to expect you back (in case something goes wrong).

2. To avoid nasty spooky areas, such as road works, big cross-roads, or the farm dog who chases horses for fun.

You will need to take a mobile phone, or money to use in a call box, and your home or yard phone number. This is in case you may need help or want to let people know that you will be back later than expected.

It is always a good idea to carry a card with your address, telephone number, and any other important details on it. (Put it in your pocket, not your hat!)

Be aware of others: give the right signals.

As ponies are not allowed on the pavement, you must now become a road user. Treat all cars, lorries and motorbikes as though they *have not seen you* and as though they have not a clue about what you will do next.

Look

Before going onto a road, or turning, or going faster, or going more slowly, or going past something scary, always look in front and behind for traffic. If there is nothing coming, signal and carry on. If there is a vehicle, wait until it has gone past.

Signal

When you make signals, make them strong, long-lasting and clear.

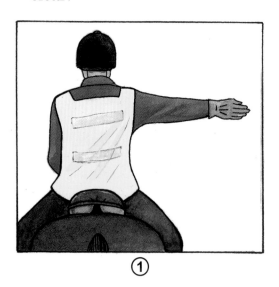
①

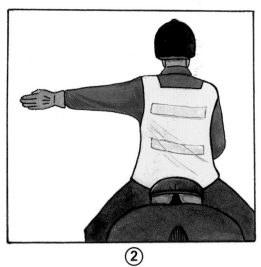
②

When you are going to move to the right or to turn right (**1**) hold your right arm out straight, and level with your shoulder. Keep your thumb tucked in so that drivers know it is a signal and not a 'thumbs up'. Hold this signal for about four seconds (while you say 'chimpanzees' to yourself.) To turn left (**2**) signal with your left arm in the same way. These are the signals used when riding a bicycle.

Never signal with your whip in your signalling hand. This may scare your pony or injure a passing pedestrian or cyclist.

Look Again

Don't move yet! After your signal, check over your right shoulder that there is no one racing up behind you. You don't want to get splattered after all that signalling. If it is safe, carry on.

LOOK   **SIGNAL**   **LOOK**   **MOVE**

Be polite to others

Most drivers are sensible when they see horses and riders. Some are kind and will stop the traffic. If this happens, say 'thank you' or give them a nod and a smile - not a little hand-wave which can leave you with less control.

In the same way, when you meet pedestrians, slow down for them and they will probably say 'thank you' to you. When there are pedestrians on a bridleway, make sure that they have seen you before you pass them. Then do so at a walk.

Ride Wisely

Defensive (Safe) Riding

Defensive riding means defending yourself from dangers on the road. Unlike a motor car, you and your pony are not protected by a big metal case, so you have to defend yourself by being sensible. You can do this by making sure that your pony has enough space and that drivers can see what you are about to do.

Ponies on the Highway

When is your pony a vehicle? The answer is: when he is on the road, or highway.

When you are using the highway, you and your pony, like other road users, must follow the rules and signs found in *Riding & Roadcraft*, which are taken from *The Highway Code*.

This means that you:
- Ride on the left side of the road
- Follow road markings
- Obey road signs
- Can ride on some rough verges
- Cannot ride on pavements or trimmed verges
- Can ride on bridleways and tracks
- Cannot ride on footpaths

Making Space

When is your pony as wide as a car? The answer is: when he is being overtaken by a car. Your position makes a difference to what cars and lorries will do around you.

If you are close to the edge (**1**) drivers are tempted to pass you. If you ride a pony's width from the edge (**2**) drivers will have to overtake you a great deal more carefully. Also, away from the edge the road surface is more even.

①

②

Changing pace in a safe place

Do ponies have a speed limit? The answer is: yes they do - so you have to go more slowly when the road is slippery or where there may be danger.

Ponies' hooves do not grip well on roads, so when turning a corner you need to walk on an even surface.

Take extra care on ice or snow. Also, be careful when walking on yellow road markings, as they are slippery.

Most riding on the road is at walk or working trot. Fast trotting will jolt your pony's legs and make him lame as he gets older. Dressage and jumping ponies need to have extra care taken of their legs.

Danger to you and your pony is where you meet other traffic. At junctions and around hazards, such as parked cars, ride at the walk.

Where the road surface is even, and straight enough for you to see traffic and for drivers to see you, you can ride at the trot.

To change pace (go faster or more slowly) you should be on a stretch of road where you can see and be seen. Look in front and behind for any traffic that might be surprised by you. Wait for traffic behind you to pass, then carry on, remembering to look behind you once again just before changing pace.

LOOK   PREPARE   LOOK   TROT

There is no safe place in which to canter. On tarmac roads, horses cannot stop easily because their metal shoes slip rather than grip. Keep fast work for fields.

Tight Turns

At junctions, give your pony room.

Ponies get scared if there are cars moving around them on all sides. The trick for keeping calm at a road junction is to take up as much space as possible.

To turn left, keep one to two horses' width from the edge of the road. Be prepared to stop and give way (the road markings shown are give way to traffic on a major road). Look behind. Give the turning left signal, then follow the Green Cross Code. Look right. Look left. Always look down your left side to see if a cyclist is coming, (lifesaver look). Look right again. Listen to make sure that all is clear. Signal left again and move off.

To turn right, keep two horses' width from the left edge of the road and indicate right. Do not use a right-hand lane if there is one; keep to the left lane. Traffic can then go to your right (your pony is used to this) but no one can sneak round on your left. This is easier for car drivers to cope with than a shivering, circling, worried pony.

Be prepared to stop and give way. Look over your right shoulder, give the turning right signal, then follow the Green Cross Code. Look behind to make sure that no one is about to overtake you. Look right. Look left. Look right again. Signal right. Move straight ahead then to the right.
NEVER CUT CORNERS.

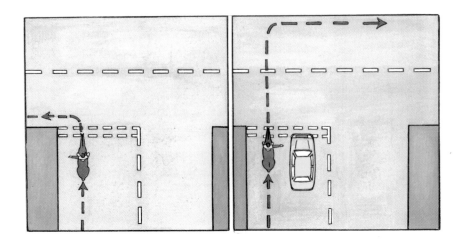

Obstacle Course

When there is something in your way you will need to go round it safely.

It may be a parked car. Is anyone at the wheel? Is it likely to move off?

It may be a hole in the road. Are there workmen in it who cannot see you?

To begin with, you will plan to leave a big gap between the obstacle and your pony, which will mean that for a short time you will be riding in the middle of the road.

As you get closer (two or three ponies' lengths) to the parked car, look behind and in front **(1)** to see what all the other traffic is doing. If there is traffic coming towards you, wait until it is clear. When it is safe to go round the car, look behind signal right **(2)** and move towards the middle of the road **(3)**. Look into the car as you go past, there might be a dog or something else which could spook your pony. Check in front and behind for any unexpected traffic. If it is safe, walk past the car, turning your pony's head away from the car, at the same time squeezing him with your right leg just behind the girth **(4)**. Thank any drivers who waited for you.

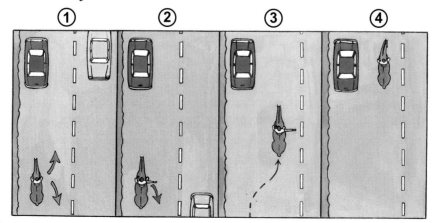

Riding Round

Roundabouts do not have to be a worry.
To get on a roundabout, treat it like a left turn at a T-junction.
Wait on the 'give way' line until the road is clear on your right (**1**).

Walk round the roundabout, staying on the left side of the road.
Watch for cars turning across in front of you (**2**). The roundabout
is like a road with lots of left turns. If you do not want to use an
exit, signal right just before you reach it (**3**). When you *do* want
to turn off the roundabout, signal left, check behind you on both
sides, and walk smoothly round the corner (**4**).

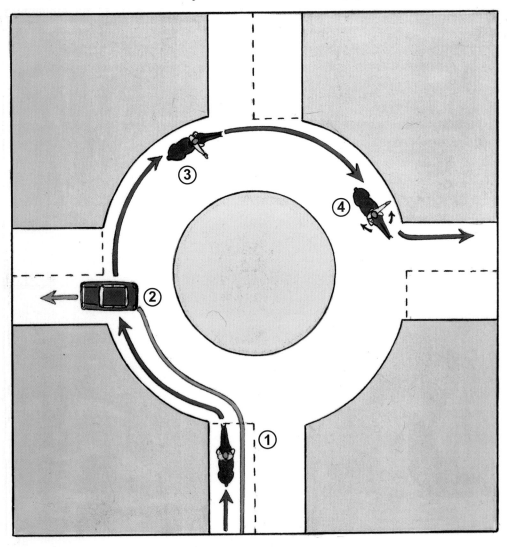

Junctions

Junctions where there are traffic lights are usually very busy and you must take extra care. Avoid them if you can. Remember that at red or amber you *must* stop **(1)**. Only at green can you move off. If you are going to turn left, look behind you, then signal **(2)**. If you are going straight ahead, there is no need to signal **(3)**.

To turn right, stay out of the way of the traffic on the left hand side. Ride across the left side of the junction and wait on the other side. When all the traffic in front of and behind you has gone past, indicate right **(4)** and turn right. By now, the traffic lights will have probably changed, so thank any drivers who have waited for you to turn.

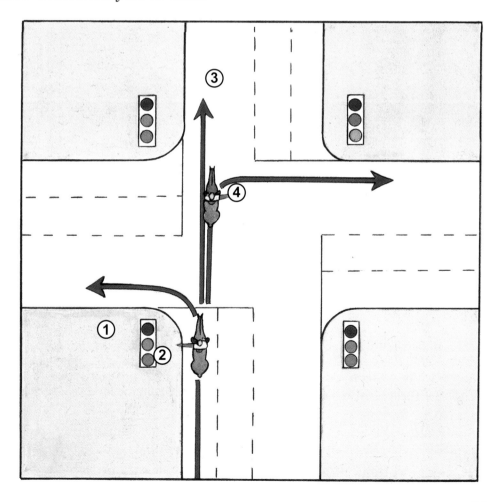

Two's Company

When riding with other people you will need to think about how to cross the road together.

You should talk to each other in good time so that you can plan what to do. It is safer to trot in single file with a gap of half to one length between each pony.

Only ride side by side where the road is wide, straight and quiet. Be prepared to go into single file the moment you hear or see any traffic coming up behind you. *The Highway Code* says never ride more than two abreast and ride in single file on narrow or busy roads or when riding round bends.

When you cross the road, you must make sure that there will be time for everyone to walk across. Ponies are herd animals and do not like to be separated from each other.

The front, and rear riders must signal clearly, and all riders should check behind them at regular intervals.

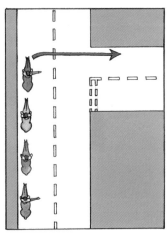

Leading your Pony on the Road

For a pony who is being led, the scary things (such as dustbins and flapping plastic sheets) don't go away, so you must both wear safe equipment. For control, your pony should wear his bridle. For your safety you must wear your riding hat, gloves, and tough, correct footwear. To be seen, you need to be in high visibility clothing.

If your pony is wearing his saddle, make sure that the stirrups are run up or crossed over.

When he is being led (**1**), your pony should walk on the left hand side of the road. You should walk next to him on his off (right) side. This means that you are between him and the traffic, which is the safest place. You can see the road ahead and behind, and motorists can see your signals. If your pony shies away from a passing lorry, he won't end up sitting on you in the ditch!

When leading, you must give any necessary signals, and look behind you at regular intervals.

If at any time you have to mount or dismount when on the road (**2**), find a place where there is plenty of room, in case your pony swings round. You could use a verge, a gateway or a bus stop. Try to keep your pony pointing in the same direction as the traffic.

①

②

Ready, Steady, Stop!

When something big and scary, such as a tractor, comes towards you, and you know that your pony will be frightened, you can ask the driver to slow down. The signal for this (**1**) is like a right turn signal. Hold your right arm out straight, with the palm of your hand facing downwards, and raise and lower it slowly a few times. The arm should be stiff right to your finger-tips.

Now and again you will have to ride *past* something that will really frighten your pony. If you know that he is about to shy, to clatter about in the middle of the road, or to gallop past, you should stop the traffic (**2**). Come to a halt a safe distance from the scary object. Look round at the driver behind you. Bring your right hand towards him, arm straight, fingers pointing up. Keep on signalling until the traffic behind you stops.

①   ②   ③

To stop traffic *ahead* of you, move out towards the middle of the road. Sit up tall. Look at the driver ahead. Raise your right hand from the elbow and push it forwards (**3**).

24

When everyone has stopped, try to get past the scary object using your right rein and right leg. When you have managed to do so, remember to thank everyone who waited for you, by nodding politely and smiling.

Slipping and Sliding

Ponies can injure themselves on slippery roads, so try not to go out in frosty weather. If you *must* ride on slippery roads, put knee boots on your pony and road studs in his shoes, and use the grass verge. If you come upon a sheet of ice, or any wet slippery surface, dismount and lead your pony across slowly. If it is too slippery for you with only two legs to control then it will be too slippery for your horse or pony with four legs with metal shoes.

If you *suddenly* find that you are on ice, drop your feet out of the stirrups and hold the reins firmly.

Look, Learn and Obey

In order to ride safely on the roads you must be able to recognise all the important road signs, markings and signals.

Signs
CIRCULAR signs give **ORDERS**
TRIANGULAR signs give **WARNINGS**
RECTANGULAR signs give **INFORMATION**

Markings
WHITE LINES either across the road or along the road give you **ORDERS and DIRECTIONS**.

Traffic Lights
These are signals at road junctions which you MUST OBEY.

On the next three pages you will find some of the most important signs, markings and signals

Signs

CIRCULAR signs giving **ORDERS**

Ahead Only

Turn left
(right if symbol
reversed)

Keep left
(right if symbol
reversed)

Route to be
used by pedal
cycles only

Mini-roundabout
(roundabout circulation
- give way to vehicles from
the immediate right)

No vehicles

No entry for
vehicular
traffic

No right turn

Manually operated
temporary 'STOP'
sign

No cycling

No pedestrians

This octagonal sign must also be obeyed

Stop and
give way

TRIANGULAR signs giving **WARNINGS**

Roundabout

Uneven Road

Road narrows on both sides

Two-way traffic straight ahead

Steep hill downwards

Wild animals

Wild horses or ponies

Low-flying aircraft or sudden aircraft noise

Other danger; plate indicates nature of danger

Cattle

One triangular sign is upside down

Give way to traffic on major roads

RECTANGULAR signs giving **INFORMATION**

Tourist attraction

Recommended route for pedal cycles to place shown

28

Markings

Lines across the road

Give way to traffic on major road

Stop at STOP line

Lines along the road

| Lane line | Centre line | Hazard warning lines | Do not cross double white lines | Do not cross solid line if it is on your side |

Traffic Lights

RED means **Stop**. Wait behind the stop line

RED AND AMBER also mean **Stop**

GREEN means you may go if it is safe to do so

AMBER also means **Stop**

Flashing AMBER means you must give way to pedestrians on the crossing, but you may continue if there is nobody crossing

If there is a **GREEN ARROW** you can go in the direction if it is safe to do so. You can do this whatever other lights are showing

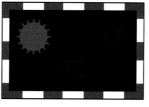

Flashing red lights mean you **MUST STOP**. They appear at level crossings, lifting bridges, airfields, fire stations

Follow the tracks (⮞, ˒, ▮) of the ponies around the village. You can see that they keep to the left except where there are hazards (❗). The squares (▬▪) tell you where to halt. The arrows (▶ ▾) tell you where and which way to signal.

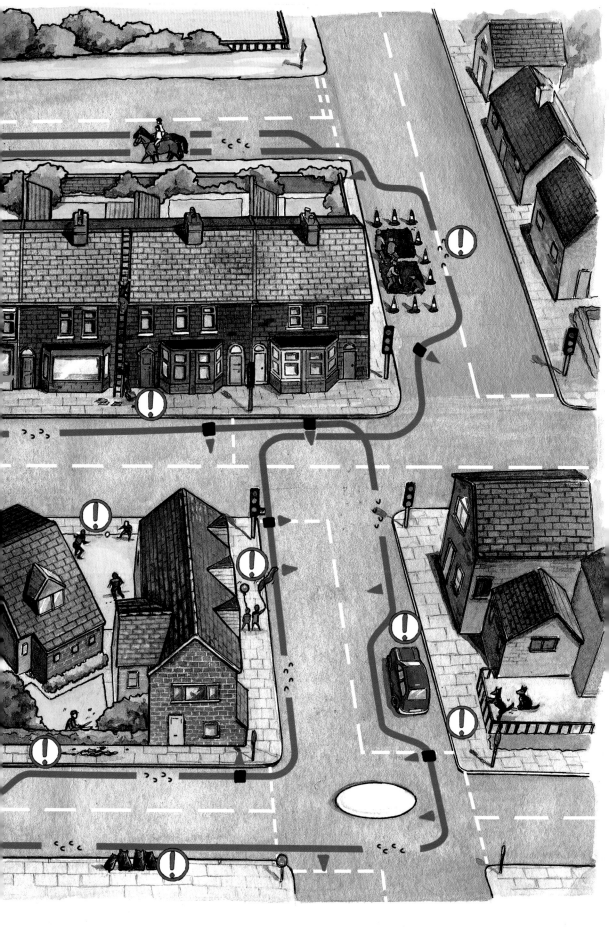

General Information

IMPORTANT NOTE

Before you can become a safe and skilful road rider you will need to study two booklets: *Riding & Road Craft*, published by the British Horse Society and *A Highway Code or Young Road Users*, produced by the Department of the Environment, Transport and the Regions. Both of these booklets contain important information from *The Highway Code*.

Where to ride away from traffic

Bridleways are tracks through fields, woods, etc., specially provided for riders (although they can also be used by walkers and cyclists). They are marked with **Bridleway** signs at each end, and you can find out where they are by checking local maps.

Byways and **Roads used as Public Paths** are road-sized tracks on which you can ride, but they are not always free from traffic.

Fields can provide safe riding areas, but you must not use them without the permission of the owners - even though you may have to go to the trouble of finding out who they are. *Do not ride* in fields where there are other animals unless you are sure that you will not scare them or that you will not scare your pony. *Never ride* over fields where crops are growing.

National Parks and **Country Parks** generally provide good routes for riders. As with bridleways, you can find out where they are from local maps. Visitors Centres have maps of their particular parks, as well as wardens who will tell you where to ride.

Fun Rides are off-road rides of 10- to 12-miles which are open to anyone, usually on payment of an entrance fee. Some provide cross-country fences for you to jump. You can find out about them from your local tack shop, or in equestrian magazines.

Further information may be obtained from your local authority's Rights of Way Officer, or from the British Horse Society Access Department, Abbey Park, Stareton, Kenilworth, Warwickshire, CV8 2XZ, telephone 02476 840500.